A ROOKIE BIOGRAPHY

LUDWIG VAN BEETHOVEN

Musical Pioneer

By Carol Greene

CHILDRENS PRESS®
CHICAGO

This book is for Charles and Kenda Webb.

Portrait of Beethoven

Library of Congress Cataloging-in-Publication Data

Greene, Carol.
   Beethoven : Musical pioneer / by Carol Greene
      p.   cm. — (A Rookie biography)
   Includes index.
   ISBN 0-516-04208-4
   1. Beethoven, Ludwig van, 1770-1827—Juvenile literature.
   2. Composers—Austria—Biography—Juvenile literature. I. Title.
   II. Series: Greene, Carol. Rookie biography.
   ML3930.B4G7   1989
   780′.92—dc20
   [B]   89-15849
                                                                  CIP
                                                               AC MN

Ludwig van Beethoven
was a real person.
He was born in 1770.
He died in 1827.
He lived a stormy life
and wrote great music.
This is his story.

TABLE OF CONTENTS

Beethoven lived in this house in Bonn, the capital of West Germany.

Chapter 1

A Sad Little Boy

In a tiny apartment
in the city of Bonn
lived a sad little boy.
His name was
Ludwig van Beethoven.

Ludwig had no friends.
No one took good care of him.
So he was messy and dirty.
He didn't do well at school.
But he could make music.

Ludwig could play
the piano and the violin.
He could make up
his own music, too.
But sometimes even music
made him sad.

Ludwig's father was
his first music teacher.
He was mean
and drank too much.
He beat Ludwig and
shut him in the cellar.

Johann van Beethoven was Ludwig's father

Sometimes he got Ludwig up
in the middle of the night
for a piano lesson.
And he didn't like Ludwig
to make up his own music.

"Silly trash!" he yelled.
"Stop fooling around!"

Maria Magdalena
was Ludwig's mother.
She died in 1787.

Ludwig's mother never
stopped his father
from hurting him.
That made Ludwig sad, too.

Sometimes he looked out
the window and thought
"lovely deep" thoughts.
They made him feel better.

But most of all,
Ludwig wanted his parents
and little brothers
to leave the apartment.

All alone, he played
the piano just for himself.
He made up music, too.
Then Ludwig was happy.

Young Ludwig (above)
played this organ (right)
at the Minorite Monastery
in Bonn when he was
nine years old.

Chapter 2

Better Times

When Ludwig was 12,
a man called Neefe
became his music teacher.
He liked Ludwig
and found him jobs.

Christian Gottlob Neefe

In those days,
Germany was divided
into many little states.
Each state had a ruler.
Each ruler had a court
with many servants.

This silhouette of
Beethoven (above) was
drawn about 1786. Ludwig
practiced on this
grand piano (right).

One of Ludwig's jobs
was to play the organ
at the court at Bonn.
Sometimes he led
the orchestra, too.

Neefe even got some of
Ludwig's own music published.

When Ludwig was 17,
his mother died.
His father kept drinking.
So Ludwig earned money
to help his brothers.

But when he was 22,
he left home.
He moved to Vienna.
It was a big, bright city.
Many musicians lived there.

Vienna was a city of music. Mozart and Haydn
lived in Vienna when Beethoven moved there.

Today some sections of Vienna look just as they did when Beethoven lived there. The royal family heard Beethoven's music at Belvedere Palace (below).

Prince von Lichnowsky was one of the
first people in Vienna to help Beethoven.

Right away, good things
happened to Ludwig.
He moved into an attic.
But a prince said
Ludwig must live with
him and his family.

He gave piano concerts
and people loved them.
Ludwig had felt sad.
He had felt happy too.
Now he put those feelings
into his music.

Joseph Haydn was
born in 1732.
He died in 1809.

He also studied music
with the great composer Haydn.
Soon people said good things
about the music Ludwig wrote.

Ludwig made many friends.
He made money too.
Each summer, he could
take a vacation
in the country.

"No one can love the country
as much as I do," he said.

But after a while,
Ludwig got tired of writing
the same kind of music.
He knew he must do
something different.

"From today on,"
he told a friend,
"I will take a new path."

Chapter 3

The New Path

Ludwig van Beethoven
was excited about
his new music.
But almost at once
something terrible happened.

Beethoven wrote
to a friend about it.
"My ears . . . hum and buzz
day and night," he said.

Opposite page: Beethoven's studio

He wondered if
he was going deaf.
A musician *had* to hear.
Beethoven kept writing music.
But he worried a lot.

Then one day, he was
in the country
with a friend.
The friend heard a shepherd
playing a flute.
Beethoven couldn't hear it.

He felt as if a storm
had burst inside him.
He said he wanted to die.
But he would not.
He would live for his music.

Beethoven wrote a letter
to his brothers.
He told them how he felt.
Then he went back to work.

He could not hear
very well with his ears.
But he could hear
his own music
inside his head.
So he went on writing.

Beethoven used these ear trumpets
to help him hear better.

Even when he took vacation trips into the country, Beethoven was writing music.

During the next eight years,
he wrote many works.
Some were for orchestra.
Some were for singers.
Some were for piano
and other instruments.

His music did sound different.
It was longer
and full of feelings.
Some people said it was
"too long" and "too noisy."
But many people liked it.

When Beethoven wasn't working,
he went out with his friends.
Mostly they talked about music.
That was how they had fun.

Sometimes Beethoven
fell in love.
He even asked women
to marry him.

But he never got married.
Deep down, he knew
that he shouldn't.
His music must
always come first.

Beethoven's home in Vienna is still standing.

Chapter 4

More Sad Times

When he was in his forties,
Beethoven went through
more sad times.
Some of his friends died.
He had money troubles.
Sometimes he was sick.

His hearing got worse too.
Soon he couldn't give
piano concerts anymore.

Beethoven wrote music for the violin.

At first he went on
writing music.
People hurried to hear it.
Kings and queens
gave him presents and
told him he was wonderful.

But then people began
to change their minds.
They wanted to hear music
by other composers.
That made Beethoven
sad and angry.

He thought about
changing his music.
It was time to take
another new path.
But he didn't know
what that path would be.

So for a while,
he didn't write much.

Karl
van
Beethoven

In 1815, his brother,
Caspar Carl, died.
He left a wife and a son.
The son, Karl, was 9.
Beethoven felt that he must
become Karl's new father.

It was not a good idea.
Beethoven didn't know
how to be a good father.
Karl was afraid of him.

Besides, Karl's mother
was still alive.
She wanted Karl with her.
But Beethoven didn't like her.
He didn't even want Karl
to see her anymore.

Everyone had a bad time.
Poor Karl went
from place to place.
Much of the time,
he lived at school.

The trouble didn't end
until Karl grew up
and joined the army.
Then at last everyone
could be friends again.

Chapter 5

Last Years

Beethoven began
to write music again.
His new music was hard
to play and sing.
But it was beautiful.

Soon he couldn't think
about anything else.
He forgot to eat.
His hair looked wild.
His clothes were messy.

One night the police
put him in jail.
They thought he was a tramp.
"That's Beethoven!"
someone told them
the next morning.

The police were sorry.
They sent Beethoven home
in a fancy coach.

Beethoven wrote this musical letter of congratulation to Archduke Rudolph on January 12, 1820.

By this time, people were
listening to his music again.
That made him feel good.

But he found out
that he couldn't lead
an orchestra anymore.
His hearing was almost gone.
That made him feel terrible.

Although he could not hear them, Beethoven would stand on the stage and watch the musicians, with his back to the audience.

One day a huge orchestra
and many singers
did one of his big works.
Beethoven stood on the stage.
He couldn't hear them.
But he watched them.

A lot of people
came to this concert.
When the music ended,
they clapped and cheered.

But Beethoven still stood
with his back to them.
He couldn't hear them either.

At last one of the singers
gently turned him around.
Then he could *see*
how much the people
loved his music.

A statue of Beethoven in Vienna

An artist drew the picture above
showing Beethoven taking an afternoon
walk through the streets of Vienna.

Beethoven couldn't hear
his friends when
they talked to him.
So he carried a
notebook with him.

His friends wrote
what they wanted to say.
Then he could answer.

42

Franz Klein made
this mask of
Beethoven.

But before long, his health
got worse in other ways.
He was in pain
and had to stay in bed.
His friends came to see him.
They brought food and gifts.

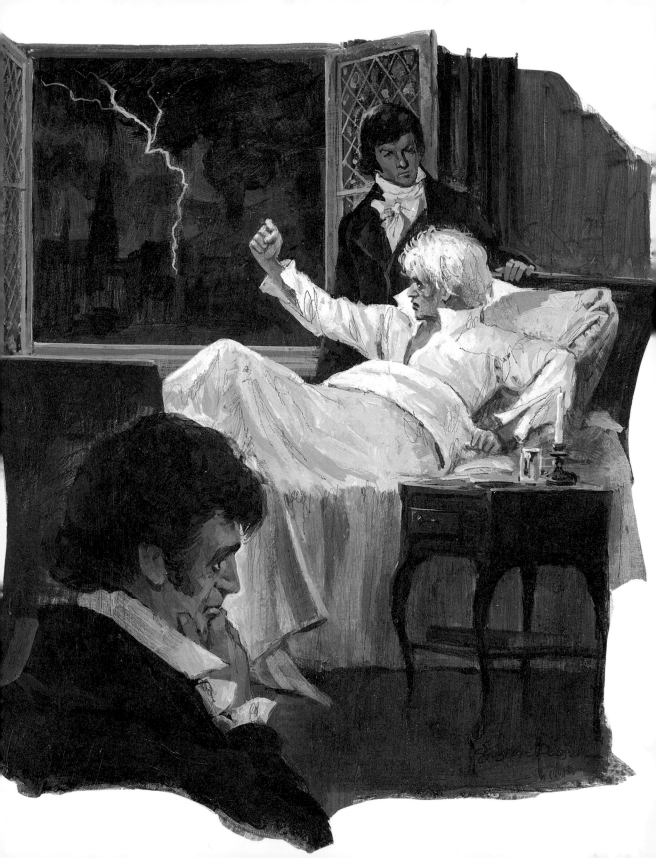

March 26, 1827, was
a strange day in Vienna.
Thunder boomed in the sky.
Snow fell on the city.

It was Beethoven's last storm.
He opened his eyes,
lifted his hand,
and made a fist.
Then his hand fell
and he died.

Important Dates

1770   December 16—Born in Bonn, West Germany, to Johann and Maria Magdalena van Beethoven

1782   Began to study with Christian Neefe

1792   Moved to Vienna, Austria

1799   Wrote First Symphony

1802   Wrote brothers about deafness (Heiligenstadt Testament)

1807   Wrote Fifth Symphony

1815   Brother Caspar Carl died

1824   First performance of Ninth Symphony

1827   March 26—Died in Vienna

INDEX

Page numbers in boldface type indicate illustrations.

PHOTO CREDITS

ABOUT THE AUTHOR

Carol Greene has degrees in English Literature and Musicology. She has worked in international exchange programs, as an editor, and as a teacher. She now lives in St. Louis, Missouri, and writes full-time. She has published more than seventy books. Others in the Rookie Biographies series include *Benjamin Franklin*, *Pocahontas*, *Martin Luther King, Jr.*, *Christopher Columbus*, *Abraham Lincoln*, *Beatrix Potter*, and *Robert E. Lee*.